Jesus Called My Name

A FAITH STORY

Fred Seiler

Seiler
Albuquerque, NM

Copyright © 2019 by Fred Seiler.

All rights reserved. No part of this publication may be reproduced, distributed or transmitted in any form or by any means without the prior written permission of the author, except in the case of brief quotations embodied in critical reviews and certain other noncommercial uses permitted by copyright law. For permission requests, contact the author.

Fred Seiler
Albuquerque, NM
www.FredSeiler@aol.com

Jesus Called My Name – A Faith Story/ Fred Seiler. —1st ed.
ISBN-13: 978-0-578-48367-2

This book is dedicated to the memory of my mother, Maria Heim-Seiler; and to my wife, Betty K. Seiler for her loving support

Contents

The Beginning 1
The War to End All Wars 10
Thou Shalt Not Have Strange Gods Before Me
.... 24
Evil Interference 26
The Move West 35
Being is More Than Life 40
May 2012 43
Interpretation 47
Epilogue 53
Parting Words 62

Acknowledgments

I am grateful to my editor, Sylvia Adamsko, a dear friend who helped me write this book.

I also want to thank the writer of "God, Dreams, and Revelations – Morton T. Kelsey - for writing his book. Also, the publisher Augusburg Fortress for giving me permission to use the quotes from Morton T. Kelsey's book.

His book inspired me and gave me the inspiration to write my book. You can find the quotes on the following pages 15, 32, 49, 54.

Introduction

This is a true story about how
I became the man that I am.
Faith in the Lord . . .

Jesus called my name.

CHAPTER 1

The Beginning

I was born March 12, 1934, to Fridrich and Maria Seiler, in the small town of Leimen, Germany. World War I had taken its toll in Europe. My father was wounded during that war. Though his legs healed fairly well, his wounds were noticeable when he walked.

For several years after he returned home, he had a difficult time finding employment. Occasionally, he worked in the forest cutting trees for firewood. Eventually, he and one of his friends decided to open a shoe factory.

When the Great Depression struck in 1929, it affected economies all over the world. Germany was not excluded. More than half the German population was unemployed and falling into poverty. My family was no exception. Business was not good and shoes were not selling. My father's shoe factory failed and once again, he was without work.

A Young Fred

Looking back on my childhood, I have no memories of playing with siblings and friends on sunny days. My youth was a time of poverty, deprivation and misery. Being the youngest of ten children left little opportunity for engaging in normal childhood activities.

My first memorable life experience happened when I was almost a year old. I remember lying on a table, surrounded by my brothers and sisters, my parents and a doctor. I was screaming like hell. My mother later told me that I'd had a very high fever. The doctor had told them I probably would not survive the illness. My parents prepared for the worst. That illness marked one of the first times God intervened in my life. Though I was too young to be aware of that, it seems I was not meant to leave this earth at such a young age.

When Adolf Hitler became chancellor in 1933 (the year before I was born), the German economy slowly began to rebound due to policies introduced by Hitler. However, in the years that followed, the economy did not improve for everyone. Privatization of state industries, tariffs on imports and reduction of foreign trade resulted in shortages of food, clothing and consumer goods that had previously been imported and readily available. Rationing of essentials did nothing to help the small, impoverished communities in Germany. I wasn't aware of most of those particular issues because I was not yet old enough to understand such things. I just knew that we were poor and that it was hard on my parents to keep all of us clothed and fed.

During those years, our family lived in a two story brick house with five bedrooms - the boys on one side, the girls on the other. We had indoor plumbing but no heat or hot water. We also had a full basement that was used to store rations for winter - things like potatoes, fruit, sauerkraut and anything else that would keep.

Ours was a typical household at that time. We lived in a mountainous area close to the French border in a town called Leimen. The town was about 3000 feet above sea level. Winters were very severe. At times, it was so cold in the house that ice would form on the inside walls and windows. Though the cold was unwelcome, it had its own special beauty when forming the prettiest ice flowers and patterns for us to enjoy.

There were mornings when I was very reluctant to leave my warm feather bed in favor of the cold. I would wait until I knew my mother had a fire going in the wood burning stove, then jump out of bed, dress as fast as I could, and race downstairs to the kitchen. It was the warmest place in the house and very large. Most of the family activities and business took place in our kitchen.

Over the next several years, my father had a difficult time finding employment. He was very outspoken against Hitler and the Third Reich. All the windows in our house were covered so no light could be seen from outside. This was because my father was meeting and talking with his friends at our house during the evening hours. They were blaming the Versailles Treaty (put into place after World War I) for the present situation. Employers did not want to risk hiring someone who outwardly did not support their German leader (despite their personal, unvoiced feelings). It was a time to be careful about who you talked to. Even a "friend" could turn you in to the authorities.

Because my father's employment was unpredictable, we were too poor to buy even basic necessities. I did not have real shoes because we could not afford them. My siblings and I would walk to school in crudely made wooden "shoes." These were strapped onto our feet by tying whatever we could find (fabric, strings and such) around the shoes to keep them on our feet. This made for difficult walking, but I was thankful to have something, anything really, instead of bare feet.

I was five years old when I began going to public school. Most of the time we sat in the school bomb shelter. When the enemy chose a target, they bombed the entire city in order to hit that target. Three years later, because it was no longer safe, the school was closed and we were all sent home.

Having her children at home kept my mother very busy. Later in life, I began to understand that it was my mother's ingenuity that helped us survive that terrible time. She did the cooking, the cleaning, the washing. She was the "Rock" in our family. When my father could not find employment, he would become very upset. My mother helped keep everybody calm as we struggled from day to day. She was also a dressmaker, working from home. No matter what the economic situation, there were always people with money who sought her out for her dressmaking skills. She made custom dresses for women who would come to the house to be measured. Most of the time, my mother would do this in the late evening and into the night. This allowed time during the day for her to tend to all the other things that needed doing to keep our family healthy. She always managed to cook a hot meal for us every evening. My mother was a truly amazing woman.

I remember everything being restricted by the Nazis - even the firewood. In the middle of the night we went into the woods to get firewood, to hunt for wild game, and collect any fruit, nuts and plants that we could eat. We were lucky to have a very large vegetable garden. It was my special responsibility to water and take care of the garden. All these tasks were done during the night. We did not want to be seen by the *Gestapo* or those in airplanes flying overhead during the day. We did not want to draw any undue attention to ourselves.

My family situation was typical of what was happening all over Germany. Many people lived in fear of what would come next. Throughout the mid to late 1930's (and continuing into the 1940's), Hitler's Nazis targeted the Catholic church (as well as its members) with false charges of "currency smuggling" and "immorality." The Nazis began dissolving anything associated with Catholicism - schools, youth leagues, workers' clubs, cultural societies, and so forth. They began to register people who went to church. The Nazis suspected that anyone who went to church had insufficient patriotism, and could not have allegiance to both the Fatherland and to God. Catholics were believed to be against Hitler because of these perceived and fragmented allegiances. The Nazis began closing the churches. Bells from the church towers were also removed and melted down to make ammunition for the military.

When I was eight years old, I served as an altar boy at our Catholic church. Every morning at 6:00 a.m., I was in the chapel; then in church by 8:00 a.m. Because of the war atrocities, many churches were closed and ransacked "for the good of Germany." Hitler's war on Catholicism led to the arrest and imprisonment of thousands of clergymen, nuns and priests in the late 1930's and early 1940's. This was when my search for God began.

I would ride my bike to a special place in the country, just outside of town. There I tried to find peace in the presence of God. I would pray and ask for answers about all the destruction around me. My deepest desire to become a priest was beginning to seem impossible during that time. I began to realize that sometimes we do not have an explanation for what moves our conscience. There is no question that such comes from wisdom beyond our own.

Life at home got worse by the day. All people received food stamps even though most of the time the stores were empty. Many times the *Gestapo* arrived unannounced to search people's houses. If they found a cow or a pig or anything that was not registered, you were in big trouble and could lose everything.

Gestapo was the shortened version of *Geheime Staatspolizei*, or Secret State Police. The term "Secret State Police" was often shortened to "*SS.*" The *Gestapo* was given carte blanche authority by the government. This allowed them to conduct their own investigations and enforce their own agenda. They could search, seize, or "investigate" any person, place or thing. They were not accountable for their actions nor were they subject to any judicial review. In short, they were virtually unstoppable.

Surviving this time was difficult. Families were torn apart. Some never recovered. The situation in Germany grew steadily worse. Meanwhile, the rest of the world was finally beginning to feel the impact as events began to escalate in Germany.

CHAPTER 2

The War to End All Wars

I was five years old when World War II began. Our world turned upside down. Many German families, like ours, were focused on survival. The events that happened next would impact my family in a way we could not have foreseen.

Not long after the war started, my oldest brother, Hugo, left for work on his bicycle, as he did every morning. On his way to work, an armored car collided with his bicycle. Hugo was killed instantly. We found out about the accident when someone from the army brought Hugo's body home. We were devastated. The army never did tell us exactly what had happened. We thought Hugo's death was suspicious. They told us there would be no further investigation. As a result, we never again heard anything more about the "accident." Instead, the army began to harass us as if we were criminals. We never fully understood why our family was being targeted; but then, not many things made much sense during that time.

My second oldest brother, Otto, was sixteen years old when he was drafted into the army. Otto was also very well educated. The *Gestapo* asked him to become a member of the *SS* and made him all kinds of promises. Otto refused their invitation. When he came home to see us, he got into an argument with my father. My father told him to never become an *SS* member and Otto agreed with him. The *Gestapo* asked Otto to become *SS* many times but he continued to refuse. As a result, the army assigned him to the front line in Berlin.

As I got older, I began to understand more about what was going on. I also began to appreciate the very real loss our family was dealing with. As the war intensified, the allies landed in France and the Russian army advanced toward Berlin.

My brother, Otto, who had been serving as a drafted German soldier, was killed. We never received his body. The army simply notified us that he was killed in combat. He was buried somewhere, but they wouldn't tell us where.

We began to fear for our safety. Bombs dropped all around us during air raids. It soon became apparent that the only thing to do was abandon our home and head for cover. My father had previously scouted the nearby forest, thinking we might need a safe place to go if we had to leave the town quickly. He found a very huge overhanging rock formation. It was about ten feet high and about ten feet square underneath. My father prepared it for our arrival.

When we fled our home in town, we grabbed what furniture and personal items we could and threw them in a wagon. We took those precious items with us as we escaped into the forest. Since we had no idea how long we would have to live there, we also took a little table, chairs, blankets to sleep on and boxes filled with food.

We called our new home a cave, but it was more like a shelter underneath an overhanging rock. The space was large enough to shelter all of us. It was also fairly well camouflaged. We cleaned out underneath the overhang to expand it for our family. It was a much safer place to live for a while.

We would sometimes sneak back to the house at night to see if it was still standing. We foraged for food in the nearby forest. Sometimes we would make our way into a farmer's fields to steal some food. I remember taking apples from a farmer's tree. They were a real treat!

We heard shooting and fighting that was only a mile or two away, but I was never afraid. We knew we had done the right thing leaving our house, but there wasn't much sleep for us in our cave. The war was so very close to where we were. It's terrifying sounds echoed across the land. My family lived in the cave for about two months. We would stay there until it was safe to return home again.

One day, my father went to the edge of town to find out what was happening. The war had advanced to our town and the German army was there and ready to fight. The American army advanced toward our town, but the Germans had built tank barriers so no one could get into town. It was a tense situation where fighting could start at any minute. All the town's people went into hiding. When my father arrived, he saw the German tank barriers at the edge of town and German soldiers who were ready to start shooting.

On one side of the tank barrier was a small opening for one man to go through. At that moment, an American Lieutenant and one soldier with a rifle came through the opening and confronted my father. Father stood his ground. The American Lieutenant wanted to make contact with the German Commander. My father took the American Lieutenant half a mile through town to the German Commander. All the town's people and German soldiers were hiding and watching to see what would happen. The Americans and the Germans came to an agreement. The German army was given 24 hours to move out.

My father then escorted the American soldiers back to the tank barriers. Not one shot was fired. If my father had run away (like anyone else might have done), the whole town would have been under fire. My father was a very brave man.

Meanwhile, allied forces advanced through France and into Germany. After about two months, things finally began to settle down in town. It was time to move back home.

We loaded our belongings on the wagon - table, stove, chairs and boxes, along with some household items and furniture. A cow was pulling the wagon and I was sitting on top of the pile. The ground we traveled over was very uneven and had lots of holes. One of the wagon wheels got stuck in a hole and the wagon overturned. I fell off and was knocked unconscious. My brother, Ludwig, found me underneath the wagon. It took him about ten minutes to get me out from under it. When he freed me, I was still unconscious. I also had a bump on my head.

At that moment, I had a beautiful out-of-body experience. I heard music that was out of this world. I found myself in glorious heavenly surroundings - joyous and peaceful. I had never before experienced anything like it. This place must have been heaven! I also sensed an unearthly, loving presence surrounding me. I can't begin to describe the elation that filled my heart. This experience still cannot be put into words almost 80 years later!

I didn't merely *believe*. I was *certain* there was a heaven; that the souls who were its citizens looked after me and thought of me as their child. This was only a prelude to greater graces yet to come. These experiences filled me with determination. They enriched and strengthened me. I still think about that long-ago vision and it continues to stay very close to my heart.

The phenomenon of out-of-body experiences can present a real challenge to our understanding; yet can be of fundamental importance to religious people. It puts into their hands a method through which they come to know and understand the depth of themselves, their faith, and glimpses of God speaking to them through those depths.

Some people use devotional meditation as a way of seeking closer relationship with God. In Christian theology, belief has it that God was - and *is* - able to speak to human beings through dreams and visions. This is also biblical and the idea persists in this age. In practice, this belief in God's revelation continues wherever people have the freedom to believe in God and worship God freely.

To have a revelation as I did at such a young age was a wonderful privilege and experience. Indeed, it is surprising how little is known about what lies beyond our modern ideas of dreams and visions.

When I regained consciousness, I was put in the wagon with my parents, brothers and sisters, and we resumed our journey home. We were happy the war was over.

Our part of Germany was occupied by the French army for a time. Two French soldiers had a room in our house and one of them played the accordion. We became good friends. That was how I was introduced to the accordion, which I still play today.

The American soldiers also treated us very well. One morning a soldier came to our house and gave my sister, Agnes, a rabbit that he had shot. (I think he liked my sister.) At that time we still had very little to eat, so the rabbit was a great joy to our family. We had meat to eat!

Across from the house where I was born, was a hotel that became the American Headquarters. One morning, I went down to the street to watch the soldiers coming and going. After a while, one soldier came towards me with a big brown bag. He put it down right in front of me. Then he turned and moved away a short distance. He watched to see what I would do with the brown bag. I opened the bag, and to my surprise, found so many goodies! There were candies, fruit, chocolate, bread, and all sorts of good things to eat. The soldier looked at me, smiled, waved and walked away. I *still* think about him today. A little goodness can go a long way.

I was eleven years old when the war ended. Because of the war, I had lost many precious years of education and development. After the war, my time was spent in evening classes, making up for the years of study I had missed out on. I also began an "on the job" training program. I found a job working for a construction company cleaning up the city. We picked up bricks and cleaned them; also glass, wood and dirt. At that time there was no schooling for me. Everyone was helping to bring the town back to its original beauty. I had that job for about two years.

When I was fourteen, I found employment in a shoe factory in another city. I got the job because of my experience working in my father's shoe factory. I worked at the shoe factory until 1957.

I was 23 years old when I decided to leave Germany and immigrate to the United States. I wanted a chance to continue my education and work toward a better future. My sister, Elizabeth, and her husband, Joe, had immigrated to the United States after the war. I stayed with them for a while, until I was able to go out on my own.

My first job in America was in a bakery on Long Island. I worked for a company that serviced the machinery the bakeries used. I worked during the night fixing their machines. Within a few months, I got a driver's license and was able to buy a car. I was proud of what I'd accomplished in such a short time – very different from the life I'd had in Germany.

From 1957-1964, I attended classes at Brooklyn Tec Evening Trade School for Tool and Dye designing. This was my formal education and I felt very grateful for the opportunity. It was also during those first few years in America that I met my wife, Hedwig. In 1964, we were married in a Catholic ceremony in New York.

By the time 1969 arrived, Hedwig and I had decided to return to Germany to live. We'd been back home only two months when my wife had to go into the hospital for cancer treatments. After a long illness, she passed away on July 30, 1982. She had suffered for twelve long years. Many times, I asked God, "Why me?" But our ways are not always God's Will.

I don't know which pain is greater, physical or mental. Before she died there were many days of hope and many days of despair. Many sleepless nights which I spent in prayer; many nights in crying or in anger. Many times I went to the doctor and inquired about her health, because one thing you cannot take away from a patient is hope. I didn't want her to know the seriousness of her illness.

When it came time to say goodbye, I told her about my experience as a teenager when I had the out-of-body experiences; how beautiful it was, how I found myself in heavenly surroundings; the music I heard and the peace that took over my whole being. Knowing the truth about life after death was a great comfort to my wife and gave her hope. This reassuring knowledge helped us accept the reality of what was happening. Death is not final. It is simply an interval before the life to come. The pain of death for those of us left behind is real; but so is the promise of the resurrection that will reunite us with our loved ones.

Before I left the hospital that evening, I had a feeling that it might be the last time I would see her and I wanted to talk with her about everything. I said to her, when she is with the Lord and I am still in Satan's domain, we should try and get in contact.

I was living alone at that time and I did not have close contact with my wife's family. Again there were many days of despair, many sleepless nights which I spent in prayer or crying in anger. I kept thinking of how we parted and the promise we'd made to get in contact *afterwards*.

For many months I felt helpless and weak. Not many people wanted to listen to me in my grief. Call it a dream or visitation: when the body lies in bed not moving, but in death-like sleep. The soul keeps awake by virtue of its own power, it imagines and beholds things above the earth, often even converses with the saints or loved ones that have passed over. It was about five months after Hedwig had passed on. Again, it happened in the morning hours. There are dreams you forget the next morning and there are dreams that stay with a lifetime.

I found myself in a huge building. It almost looked like a sanatorium, very quiet and peaceful. The room had all glass walls and you could look inside. The spirits inside did not walk, they floated, and I could not recognize any faces. They all had an aura around their heads.

One spirit followed me from room to room until a very huge man approached me. I asked him if I could get a room because it was very nice and peaceful there. The very friendly man said "No! You do not live here. Let me show you where you live." He took me to a door that led outside, bending over a balcony and pointing down. In that instant, I could see the Earth; the light, the water and the five continents. It was a beautiful sight.

That again was a vision that I could never forget. Is it possible I was in purgatory looking for my wife? It is reasonable to suppose that this applies to the case of dying and coming to life so that the dead return to life just as the living die? If this were not so, if the process of dying was not reversible, life would ultimately vanish from the universe.

My next experience happened about one year later.

I found myself in a wondrous valley looking up the hill at a beautiful mansion. I could see, hear and feel. The first thing that happened was a little girl about five or six years of age jumped up and held me around my neck like she had known me all my life. I picked her up, but she had no weight. Before I realized it, I was up the hill at the mansion. There were no windows, no doors; but there were beautiful flowers, bushes and trees that I have never seen before. We went inside and I found myself standing before my wife. I will not pretend to know something I have not experienced. At that moment I knew my body was lying in bed and sleeping; yet I could see, feel and hear her. My wife said we could not have children on earth, but she was taking care of one in heaven. At that moment, the very desires and intuition of my inmost heart assured me that another and more lovely land awaited me; an abiding city.

The reality of our experiences of the non-physical is supported by a basic religious view of the universe and having known it in simplest terms. This theory sees human beings in touch with a spiritual world that is just as real as the physical world revealed by our five senses.

As time passed on, I felt like something had been taken away from me. I was living alone and for a while, I lost my direction and this was how I wound up in the New Age Movement.

CHAPTER 3

Thou Shalt Not Have Strange Gods Before Me

For an understanding of this commandment, we must know how it was violated. Some people worshiped demons. Even now, there are many who transgress this commandment; such as those who practice fortune telling.

Such things, according to Saint Augustine, cannot be done without some kind of pact with the devil. Some worship the heavenly bodies, sun, moon, and stars instead of the Creator who made them.

The astrologers sin against this commandment by saying that these bodies are the rulers of souls, when in truth they were made for the *use* of man whose sole ruler is God. Some people worship their ancestors. Some idolize or worship men who made a great impression in their lives. This is where I fell into the trap.

About twenty years ago I was introduced to the New Age Movement. They talked about the sun, moon and stars and people I never heard of. In fact, they worshiped these people. I attended conventions and became a member of this movement. I purchased books and other materials and followed their practice. This lasted two years until I realized that I had made a terrible mistake. In fact, I had violated the Ten Commandments in many ways.

I was a widower at that time. I had become a real liberal and did whatever made me feel good. When I realized my mistake, it was like an inner voice talking to me. "Freddy, wake up! You are on the slippery slope down to hell."

Realizing my life had become so smooth; I thought, I'm not being tempted at all. Then it dawned on me that I was no longer in the battle! Satan was not worried about me anymore.

It took me about a week to finally get up the nerve to speak to a priest about my involvement in the New Age Movement. I went to confession, canceled my membership in the group, destroyed all books and materials and asked God for forgiveness.

The cleverest trick of the devil is to convince us that he doesn't exist. From that day on, my life was changed.

CHAPTER 4

Evil Interference

*"Now war arose in heaven.
Michael and his angels fighting against
the dragon; and the dragon and his
angels fought, but they were defeated
and there was no longer any place
for them in heaven."*

Rev 12:7-8

The devil and his fallen angels must have all fallen to earth, where they are still today. From that day on, I was physically attacked. It happened when I was asleep or awake. One time he picked me up and threw me against the bedroom wall. Another time he was right on top of me and strangled me. I must have done something right to get the devil that angry.

Things got so bad that I was afraid to go to bed and was afraid for my life. I called the priest and had the house blessed and called on Jesus every time I was attacked.

Later however, through these attacks of the devil, I could feel another presence near me that interfered as soon as another attack approached. Believe me, the devil is real.

After my encounter with the devil, I joined a charismatic prayer group within my parish. We met every Monday night. This made me feel so good and there was finally peace in my life. I made a commitment to stay away from bars, night clubs and other questionable entertainment. I made a 180 degree turn.

One night our leader of the prayer group decided we were going to pray for the Holy Spirit, and in a month's time, the priest would be present celebrating Mass with Holy Communion.

Before that special day, however, I had a terrible accident while driving home from work. Both cars were totally destroyed and on fire, but the other male driver and I both walked away without a scratch. This was a miracle.

Since I could not be present for the special evening because I had no transportation, I stayed at home. Around 9:00 pm, my nerves were restless and

I could not sleep. I decided to finish a book I was reading.

> *I went to get the book. Knowing where it was, I did not turn on the light. When walking into the room, it lit up by itself. I did not know what to think in that instant. I went to the window to see where the light was coming from. It was pitch dark outside.*
>
> *I looked toward the sky and at that moment it was like a window had opened up and a beam of light came into my room. This happened for one brief moment and after that, I was standing in a darkroom again.*

I only know something very extraordinary happened to me. I went down on my knees and tears came running down my cheeks. Then I remembered the prayer group at church that evening. Is it possible the Holy Spirit came to me that evening? It took me several hours to compose myself.

A week later I spoke to my priest and asked his opinion. He said that since I could not be there that evening, the Holy Spirit had come to me.

I've been a widower for seven years by that time and was tired of being alone, but afraid of getting married again because fifty percent of marriages end in divorce.

Again, I turned to God for direction and help. I asked God to lead me to the right person to spend the rest of my life with. I made a commitment to pray for half an hour every morning and evening. I even told God what I was looking for in a wife.

After about six months, one morning, I was too tired to get up when the alarm clock went off. I reached over to shut the clock off and stayed in bed. In that instant, a man's voice came through the whole house. "Fred, you are not coming this morning?"

I jumped out of bed!

About a month later, after leaving Germany, I met my present wife, Betty, under such circumstances as you can only say "Thank you, God!"

In 1987, when I moved back to the United States, I bought a house in Saint James, Long Island, New York. It was a very nice, small suburban town with only one traffic light, beautiful private beaches and parks.

I was working for *Grumman Aircraft* and everything was going my way. Then news came that the company had lost their contract with the Navy. About ten thousand people lost their jobs. One day, I had to work late to finish an assignment and I was one of the last ones to leave the company. I had to drive five miles up to the highway. As I was making my right turn into the highway, my car stopped and I was just able to get off the road. I was getting out of the car and I said out loud, "Tonight I need a miracle to get home."

Just as I had finished the sentence, a car pulled right behind me. The driver asked if he could help me. He pulled my car five miles back to the company where I could get a loaner car to get me home. As I turned around to thank him, he left. That man came from nowhere and went into nowhere. Was it an angel? I have no other explanation. This was a wonderful and timely experience. How precious to know our guardian angels are ever with us.

At that time, I attended a neighborhood parish which offered classes in basic theology. In one of these, I became involved in a conversation with our teacher and we were talking about the Mother of God. When I mentioned that I was saying the rosary frequently, she looked at me and asked if I believed in witchcraft. I was so shocked that I had no answer. Later I found out that she was not a Catholic. But for me, that was no excuse.

At the time, I worked for Grumman's with a few friends of mine. We all met in the boss's office with his secretary once to pray the rosary. Because of my faith, I just couldn't let that comment about witchcraft go by and not do something about it.

The following Sunday, I went to Mass because I wanted to speak with the priest. I wanted to tell him who was teaching basic theology in his parish. Knowing he was hearing confessions before Mass, I made sure that I got to speak with him. He was very surprised and thanked me for telling him. After our conversation, the priest went to the altar and started Mass.

Before we received communion, we prayed the Our Father and, after that, the priest was wishing everyone God's peace. The congregation then shook hands with everyone around them. I turned around to wish God's peace to the people behind me. There was a lady I'd never seen before, more beautiful than anyone I had seen in my life. She wore a long gown and long gloves with a veil over her head, which covered her whole face. She took my hand in both of hers. I felt the pressure in my hand and the only thing I could see through her veil were her eyes.

After wishing peace to all the people around me, I could not resist the urge to look back once more to see who was standing behind me, but there was no one there.

Even today, thinking about that vision and asking myself if it was the Mother of God, I will never forget the beautiful lady that Sunday morning.

A dream is not a small thing. It can be a revelation and a sure sign from God, as we know from the New Testament and from the dreams of Abimelech, Joseph and Daniel. Dreams can be given for the common good as well as for personal direction. Even today I think about that vision and ask myself if it was the Mother of God. I will never forget the beautiful lady that Sunday morning.

My Beautiful Lady

When news came out about *Grumman Aircraft*, that we were all going to lose our jobs in about a week, I had another dream.

I found myself in New York City, running through the streets with a friend, looking for protection. Most buildings and high-rises were destroyed. There was no electricity. It was a real disaster and everyone was looking for protection. As I looked toward the sky, I saw a beautiful cross lit up, and the next moment the cross vanished and Jesus Christ appeared in all His glory.

The next morning many thoughts went through my mind. Was it possible that God was telling me to leave the city? Knowing that I was going to lose my employment and was close to retirement, I shared the dream with my wife, Betty, and it was she who had no problem believing that the dream had come from the Holy One.

CHAPTER 5

The Move West

In about a year's time, we put the house on the market. In one month, the house was sold when no one else could sell their homes. We moved from Long Island to Albuquerque, New Mexico which has a warm, dry climate. It also has a very good retirement community. We purchased a house near the Sandia Mountains which overlooks the entire city.

The first thing I did after retirement was build a garden house in the back yard for my hobbies and woodcarving. It was a time when my wife went to work and I was home alone.

I came across a book about Saint Therese of Lisieux. I was very impressed with the story of her short life on earth and how she served God in her 'little ways.' Before she passed on to heaven she said "I want to spend my time in heaven doing good on earth. I cannot rest as long as there are souls to be saved, until time is no more."

In that little book, there are certain prayers and novenas to be made to Saint Theresa as an intercessor. So I decided to make a novena. One novena is said with certain prayers for five days in a row, before 11:00 AM. On the fifth day, you say them twice. The night after I finished my novena, I had a beautiful dream.

> *Saint Theresa came to me in a dream with a beautiful bouquet in her hands which she gave to me. When she walked away from me, I called after her, "Wait, I want to go with you." But she turned and said, "No. Where I go, you cannot come yet."*

Again, it was a dream, so beautiful that I cannot describe it with words. My body was lying asleep, yet my soul was seeing and conversing with Saint Theresa.

In the passing months I kept thinking about the beautiful dream until I had an idea, wondering what would happen if I made another novena? I started a new novena and while doing so, kept thanking her for that beautiful dream I'd had. Again, I said my prayers before 11:00 AM and along came the fifth day. I was watching TV at 10:00 AM when I realized I had to finish my novena. I shut off the show I was watching and went to my room to finish the novena.

I finished about 10:40 AM and decided to watch the end of the TV show.

I went back to turn on the color TV. The picture came on, but instantly the picture went out and Saint Theresa appeared in black and white for half a minute with a rose in her hand. She left, and the picture came back on again.

Do you have any idea how I felt? I could not move for quite some time.

It is now several years later, but in my mind it is like this happened yesterday. Sometimes I wanted to share my experiences with a friend, but most of them do not listen with an open heart and often walk away from me. Many times you lose your friends. I like to share my story with other people and tell them to be careful: hell, purgatory and heaven are real. But unfortunately, most responses are very negative.

Our theology shows us that gifts are not given to enrich the people who receive them. They are a gift for the entire church. This is the reason why God created the universe; to give us a share in himself during our life on earth.

St. James urges us to be doers of the Word and not hear it only. Well, I tried a few times in my life, when I was growing up in Germany. There was the war and my wish to become a priest was not possible. Later, after retirement, I tried to be a deacon but was not accepted. Why? Only God knows. So I just had to live my life like St. Theresa of Lisieux and try to do God's work in little ways. I finally become a Prison Minister. I would go every Sunday morning to the prison to give Catholic communion services. I did this for ten years.

One year ago, my brother-in-law, Jim, came to live with us in Albuquerque. Jim was injured in an accident years before, which left him with a crushed spine. He suffered with pain for years and this led to drug and alcohol problems. My wife and I were hoping to help him overcome these problems but Jim had a mind of his own. He wanted to do things his way. Apparently his way was not the best way. Jim passed away too soon. He was only 56 years old.

Jim was a very goodhearted person. He trusted everyone he met. Unfortunately, our society got the best of him. We had a Memorial Mass for him in the Catholic Church. Jim was cremated and buried in a Catholic cemetery. We know he moved on to a better place, but we are left behind with sadness and helplessness.

CHAPTER **6**

Being is More Than Life

I know three things: that Jim is dead; that whatever a man suffers in this world, there is an end to suffering; and that all the pain and trouble of this world have an end.

How God will judge Jim, I do not know. But I know Jim had a good heart and many times he quoted the Bible to me. My wife and I are very sad that Jimmy has left us, but I would like to tell you how Jim contacted me for the past three months.

Many people want to know about interpretation of dreams. Sometimes dreams speak with a clarity that can scarcely be missed; but often, they speak in the language of pictures. If we wish to understand dreams we must first be serious seekers for deeper meanings in life and deeper contact with God than most people have.

After Jim passed over, he came to me in a dream a month later.

> **I was out in the countryside like I was waiting for someone. There came Jim. He was dressed very nicely. I recognized him right away and told him so. He did not speak to me but we enjoyed each other's company.**

In the second dream:

> **Jim came to the house. He rang the doorbell. Again, I recognized him. I told him I had to get the key for the gate. When I returned with the key he was gone.**

I feel these contacts came from Jim. He wanted us to know that he was still with us. I believe very strongly in hell, purgatory and heaven.

Jim remained four months in purgatory. On June 28th, he came to say goodbye. I had no problem understanding because that dream was guided by the Holy Spirit.

In the Bible, Joseph was asked to interpret dreams. He replied, "Do not interpretations belong to God?"

On June 28th in the morning hours, I cannot tell you if I was asleep or awake when I had this dream:

> ***A ball of white light appeared in my room. It was a light brighter than the sun, but I had no problem looking into it. Jim was standing right in the middle of the light. He wore a long white robe and had an aura around his head. This vision lasted about two seconds. Instantly I was shown the night sky with all the stars.***

To me, that dream is self-explanatory. I am very happy for Jim – that his life of misery and disappointments is over. I am looking forward someday to meeting him again. God Bless You, Jim.

CHAPTER 7

May 2012

An inner voice is telling me to continue to write down my further Dreams and Experiences. However, as I listened to my dreams, I found a Presence wiser than me, trying to guide me through my difficulties to holiness; a holiness that was possible only when I continued to be touched by the Infinite.

Jesus said, one time, "If you don't become like little children, you will not go into heaven" (*not* childish, child-like). If I tell little children a story about heaven, God and the Angels, their eyes light up and they get very excited. Children have no problems believing. They already know what Jesus meant when he said, "Like little children."

Am I at that point? I saw the light come into my room from above, shook hands with a beautiful lady in church, who vanished; and, in the next second, saw my wife in heaven after she had passed on. I think I got the message that God was there and I was going in the right direction. I only wished that the Christian community had been there to guide me on the journey.

I will tell you of a man in Germany and about Hitler, so you may understand how important it is to share our dreams and messages from God.

Martin Niemollen was confronted in a dream with the light of God. He heard the voice of Hitler behind him saying, "Martin, Martin, why didn't you ever tell me?" He awoke and realized that he was not faithful to his God! Martin had been face-to-face with Hitler many times and never shared his convictions about Jesus with Hitler. He then spoke out on the faithlessness of his church in Nazi Germany.

Are we paying any attention to our dreams today? Today there is no room for these dreams in our materialistic and logical world. When Jesus left this earth after his resurrection, he said, "I will go and prepare a place for you."

God made man in his image; and for us to be with him after our trials on earth. Why does God send me that following dream? I do not know! Dreams and visions do not reveal the nature of God, but they are given by him. Referring to a dream that brought convictions about life after death, God can use a dream as a vehicle of revelation to a soul. It can be a vehicle of revelation from God if a person's life is turned toward God.

God sent me a vision:

> *I was standing in the front entrance of a house. The entrance was very impressive, but I only saw the entrance; and next to the entrance was my family name, "Seiler." The name above Seiler was not legible. One week later, I had the same vision again. I was standing at the same front entrance and two people came out. One spirit said to me, "Are you ready for the next assignment?"*

All men are guided by their own minds. There are some few who are worthy of divine communication. So what will my next assignment be? I hope that God will reveal it to me! What impact that can have in a man's life!

A week ago I had to go into the hospital for a pacemaker. Before the nurse gave me the anesthesia, I thought about what I saw, heard and experienced. A certain calm and peace came over me. It showed me that a dream was a significant religious truth that could be seen and interpreted.

CHAPTER **8**

Interpretation

Jesus said, "I will send you the comforter" (the Holy Spirit). And so God's Spirit is poured out in dreams and visions.

What do I understand? The whole year we go to church and pray for the Holy Spirit; but you will find very little understanding to share your belief, dreams and supernatural experiences with other parishioners.

There are many dreams that you do not remember the next morning, but when that Spirit speaks to you, then you know you had a vision.

I had two dreams; and since I had these dreams, my understanding is that they came from Jesus. I will try to tell you them as honestly as I can with my little mind and worthless soul.

My first encounter started in the morning hours finding myself in a quiet and peaceful surrounding. Then I realized someone wanted to put his arms around me. I moved away from him and said very angrily, "I am not a queer." He smiled at me and said, "I know you are not a queer." We walked together a short distance and again he smiled at me and said, "I take care of you" and vanished. Then I realized it was Jesus.

I experienced the presence of a loving God who wished to draw us closer to him. What can I say so that you believe! Maybe you should pray and ask for wisdom and understanding.

My second vision happened a month later. I have to start by saying I never expected to experience this or to have this happen.

In the second vision, I saw the crucifixion of Jesus Christ. I was shown how they stretched him out on the cross and nailed him. Everything was so realistic it was like being there . Then the vision vanished and Jesus came to me and said,

"I died for you, Friedolin."

Friedolin is the name I was baptized with and I only use it for important documents. Fred is the name I go by, knowing there is nobody out there who believes me because revelation and inspiration through dreams is a dead issue for Christians in our time.

There have been several reasons for not paying attention to dreams. There is material reality and consciousness and nothing else.

Certainly man can teach man when he is awake and attentive. However, God can instruct very effectively in a dream when man is sleeping. That will never take away the knowledge that came from God. Once the spirit is separated from the body and relaxed, then dreams or revelations can come to you. These dreams and revelations will be much easier and far superior to any teaching from man.

For several centuries after the dark ages, in western Europe, the people had not been either

Christian or literate where Greek culture and the spiritual leaders of the Eastern Church continued to flourish.

After the fall of Constantinople, many manuscripts and scholars came to the West. Then serious studies of dreams once again emerged.

A special priest that comes to mind is Don Bosco, who was guided by dreams and told by the Pope to write everything down.

We have far more capacity than we realize. When I puzzle over a dream, I spend more time with the Holy One.

When I had the dream about the crucifixion of our Lord Jesus Christ, I know that dream was given to me from none other than the Holy Spirit, whom God gives us as our inner guide, friend and comforter.

Most Christians think dreams and visions went out with the dark ages and that there is no need to think about them. But the early Christian Church found dreams and visions most important up to the time of Aquinas. And what has happened to our dreams and spirituality today?

At the parish I belong to, I sang in the choir. But for some time, I was not very happy about the way people behaved in church. I grew up with the old traditional Mass where people were quiet and dressed properly and received the host from the priest kneeling down at the altar. Like I said, I started to sing in the choir, near the altar. I saw the people coming to the altar to help the priest give communion. Some of the women were in shorts and loose blouses with no sleeves and men were in shorts. (O my God, have mercy on us.)

Then the choir started to sing, but it was so loud, that there was no meditation and reflection on our Lord possible. In our church today on Easter and Christmas, the church is full. Throughout the year not even half of the community shows up. Is this what Jesus calls the "lukewarm" that he said he will spit out? It is very sad to see that most people use all their time and energy and resources for this life that will vanish and has no eternal value.

You might ask me why I get these dreams. God knows me better than I know myself, and I believe in the Holy Spirit, which we pray for every day in the Apostle's Creed.

What I have written down is the truth. And what can I say that people will believe me? There is a saying,

"When the heart is full,
it is running over."

I wanted to share my experiences with everybody.

Four times I wanted to become a deacon, but I was rejected, because they did not believe me. The people I met in the churches made fun of me. So now I am putting all my trust in Jesus, because he said to me when he came to me the first time,

"I will take care of you."

Now that you have read my biography I hope that you have an open mind. Many people that I shared my experiences with have walked away from me.

Why should dreams be given by God to obscure and uneducated men and not the learned?

God does give revelations and dreams to the uneducated, if only to show that the learning of worldly people can cut them off from the higher pursuits; also to show that piety is superior to knowledge.

CHAPTER 9

Epilogue

To the early Christian church Fathers, dreams and visions were very important and significant. We believe that dreams are sent by God and by evil spirits. Human beings have eternal destinies in the world, that are revealed by dreams.

Mid-February, 1992

One night I had a dream that I was standing in my backyard and there were black clouds laying on top of the houses. Flames of fire were shooting through the clouds. It was very frightening because I had also "seen" the destruction of the

Twin Towers in Manhattan before it happened in 2001.

For this reason, I hoped what I saw in my backyard (that February night) would never come true.

I have come to see the value and significance of dreams. In dreams we already have direct spiritual communication with non-physical realities. I never ask to see that. The dreams are just given to me.

The soul reveals a spiritual reality. It is evidence for the immortality of the soul. We see sleep as a time of special receptivity for discovering the soul's destinies.

In my prayer life, I pray for the souls in purgatory. I found myself in a very desolate place. People were living in caves and were very afraid to be seen. It looked to me as if demons and evil spirits were controlling the area.

Three people came up to me: two men and a woman.

They asked me for help! I felt that I was in purgatory. The men and woman did not give me their names, but I felt as if they knew me and were asking me for help!

So I went to the priest and had a Mass said for the three people I'd met in purgatory.

A month later, in a dream, a woman came to me with bandages all over her body. She was looking very happy. She thanked me. She was moving on.

In some dreams, people may have certain things pointed out to them. What I am now writing, I swear by God, that it is the truth.

At the end of March 2016, at 3:00 AM Something woke me from my sleep. A voice spoke to me and told me to go outside. When I went outside, I looked toward the sky. I could not believe what I saw with my own eyes. It was an object moving over the horizon, about ten times the size of the full moon. I could see that the object had three dimensions. The whole object was lit up in all colors imaginable. In my amazement I did not know what to think! Standing there, I made the sign of the cross to let them know that

Jesus was my savior.

I ran inside the house to get my wife so that she too, could see. But it was too late. The object was gone.

One month before the alien spaceship appeared, two aliens appeared in my bedroom.

The aliens were standing at the foot of my bed on the right-hand side. When they realized I'd awakened and noticed them, they vanished through the walls. A week later, one alien spirit appeared to me in my dream. I screamed at him to leave me alone.

Then my guardian angel appeared and the alien vanished.

Revelations vs 13

Therefore rejoice, ye heavens,
And ye that dwell in them.
"Woe to the inhabitants of the earth
And of the sea!
For the devil is come down into you,
having great wrath
Because he knoweth that he hath but
A short time.

June 17, 2017

Many people I talk to don't believe, and I know they are having a problem with that. Christians who wish to understand, need to learn from their dreams. They must learn to appreciate the images and symbols those dreams contain. Only then can they be on the path to knowing.

For many years my wife, Betty, and I have talked to God before we go to bed. We talk about our problems and wishes and thank him for being our Father. We close with a prayer for the poor souls in Purgatory.

The dream I had on June 17th started with a group of 25 people standing in a desolate area. I was standing with them. They were waiting for a person that suddenly appeared. She started talking to the group of people and pointing to me, saying, "He is your helper out of purgatory". She mentioned only the family name SEILER.

That dream is self-explanatory and we are very grateful.

July 16, 2017

I dreamed I was sitting in a church and had the bible lying next to me. Suddenly, a man sat down next to me, pointed to my bible and asked if he could have it. I gave it to him with the hope that he would return it. After a while, I asked for the return of my bible because I was going to leave the church. He said, "No," and wanted to keep it. This was when I realized he was Putin, the Russian President.

There is a saying, "Never say *NO* to your mother." However, the Vatican said "NO" to our Mother in Heaven. They did not attempt the conversion of Russia. The message of Fatima was virtually ignored. And we have seen the consequences of the First World War: moral collapse in every society; the plague of Fascism and Nazism. The Second World War claimed 60 million lives. My family and I survived in a cave in the mountains. Now we have widespread abortion. Families are breaking down. Many leaders are talking about Armageddon. Why doesn't the Pope make the consecration to Russia so Russia will be converted? Then Putin can read the Bible.

One can determine whether the dream has been sent by God and believed. Inner illumination of the soul can be powerfully conveyed to others. The Vatican missed the biggest opportunity in history to save mankind from destruction, and Russia would have been converted to Christianity. What a shame! Only a few will reach heaven in the time we are living in. The rest will have to go to purgatory. Sadly, many people will die and leave no one behind to pray for them.

Referring back to March 2016, I am sure the space ship made the connection: From God the creator, his Son, Jesus Christ and the cross. When the aliens saw me making the sign of the cross, they left me. The next morning I was still all bewildered. I went outside in my backyard. Almost the whole lawn was burned and destroyed.

I knew my privacy was invaded. Life after that was not the same anymore.

Europe at one time was the cradle of Christianity. Look at the beautiful churches and cathedrals that were built in Europe. The churches were filled with worshipers.

In 1917, the Mother of God came to Fatima. She appeared to three little girls and asked them to go to the bishop and ask him to go to the Pope. The message was to make the consecration of Russia. But the Pope had no time to listen to heaven. He went into politics. Now the church of Christ is still threatened by three enemies: Russians, Communism, and Liberalism. These three are cooperating united against God and his church. God Help Us!

February 10, 2018

One night a voice came to me—ugly and straight from hell. The voice said in German,

"*Kiss My Ass.*"

I assume he knows me and is asking for my help.

CHAPTER 10

Parting Words

I consider my little book to be completed.

What can be more beautiful and gratifying than Jesus coming to me in a dream and saying,

"*I died for you, Friedolin.*"

Friedolin is the name I was baptized with.

I decided to write down what I feel is important to me. The soul grows upward and finds the fulfillment of something implanted in its nature. This evidence is capable of grounding reasonable and responsible belief in a super intelligent God.

God created our universe.
Our universe is 13.7 billion year old
and 13.7 billion light years radius.
Is that a coincidence?
I do not think so!

Now that you have read my biography, I hope that you have an open mind. Many people that I have shared my experiences with have walked away from me.

Why should dreams be given by God to obscure and uneducated men and not the learned?

God does give revelations and dreams to the uneducated, if only to show that the learning of worldly people can cut them off from the higher pursuits; also to show that piety is superior to knowledge.

What can I say about what I have seen? Well, that is easy to answer,

Because what I have seen, I have seen.

God bless you all.

www.ingramcontent.com/pod-product-compliance
Lightning Source LLC
Chambersburg PA
CBHW041352290426
44108CB00001B/19